Earth Sun iron tree roots plates frog

earthquake canyon volcano lava child

mountain valley rock diamond cave ash

miner coral reef polar bear tornado

desert rainforest flooding penguins zebra

fish meerkats starfish lightning

Our Earth

Written by Janine Amos
Reading consultants: Christopher Collier and Alan Howe,
Bath Spa University, UK

First published by Parragon in 2008
Parragon
Queen Street House
4 Queen Street
Bath BA1 1HE, UK

ISBN 978-1-4075-5822-6

Printed in China

Our Earth

Bath · New York · Singapore · Hong Kong · Cologne · Delhi · Melbourne

Contents

Our planet

The Earth is a huge ball of water, soil and rock. It is surrounded by air.

You cannot feel it, but the Earth is always moving. In one year, it travels completely round the Sun. At the same time, it also spins like a top.

The Earth is tilted. As it moves, places on the Earth get different amounts of sunlight. This gives us the seasons.

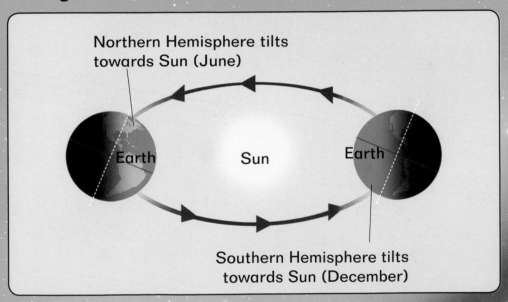

Northern Hemisphere tilts towards Sun (June)

Earth

Sun

Earth

Southern Hemisphere tilts towards Sun (December)

The Earth makes one complete turn every 24 hours. It is daytime when our side of the Earth faces the Sun.

The Earth's layers

The Earth has layers like an onion. The outside layer is made of rock. Inside this there are rock and metal.

The thin outside layer of our Earth is called the crust. Inside this is the mantle, made of hot rock and metal. At the centre lies Earth's metal core – the hottest place of all.

crust

core

mantle

The iron in the Earth's metal core makes it a giant magnet.

The Earth is wrapped in an invisible cloak of air called the atmosphere. The air we breathe in, and then breathe out, comes from the atmosphere.

The atmosphere has five different layers stacked one on top of the other.

Exosphere
800 KILOMETRES

Thermosphere
700 KILOMETRES

Mesosphere
80 KILOMETRES

Stratosphere
50 KILOMETRES

Troposphere
20 KILOMETRES

EARTH

Our moving Earth

The Earth's crust is cracked into massive pieces, like a huge jigsaw puzzle. These pieces are called plates. They are always on the move.

There was once one huge area of land on the Earth's surface.

200 million years ago

About 200 million years ago it began to split in two.

155 million years ago

About 60 million years ago the two parts broke again, and today's continents were formed.

60 million years ago

As the Earth's plates move and grind past each other they can get stuck. The ground shudders – it's an earthquake!

Most earthquakes are gentle. But others can destroy buildings and harm the people inside them.

The picture below shows the crack at the point where two plates meet in Iceland.

Volcanoes

A volcano erupts when the great plates making up the Earth's surface pull apart. Hot melted rock spurts out from inside.

When a volcano erupts, red-hot melted rock called magma escapes from inside the Earth. As it cools it gets hard.

Volcanoes produce not just magma but also huge clouds of dust and ash.

Big, violent eruptions happen when thick magma clogs up the top of a volcano.

Amazing!

Magma that has reached the surface of the Earth is called lava.

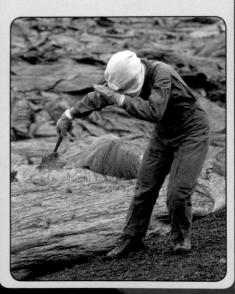

Mountains and rivers

When the Earth's moving plates bump against each other, the Earth's surface folds and crumples, or cracks. Mountains and valleys are made.

When the Earth's plates bump and squeeze together, the crust is crumpled into mountains.

The Himalayas in Asia are the world's highest mountains.

The movement of the plates makes valleys and canyons in the Earth's surface. Rivers may flow through them.

Volcanoes can also create mountains. Layers of erupted rock build up to make tall, cone-shaped mountains.

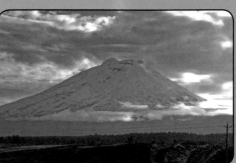

Amazing!

The Andes in South America is the longest mountain chain on land. It stretches for 7200 kilometres.

Rocks and soil

Rocks cover the Earth's surface. Although some rocks are very hard, they can be changed over many years.

Tree roots spread and split rocks apart. Small animals burrow and force rocks to crack.

Rainwater mixed with acid from the soil soaks into the ground. It can wear away rock to make underground caves.

Metals, such as silver and gold, and rare stones, such as diamonds, are found in some kinds of rocks.

Miners dig into the Earth to find minerals, precious metals and rare stones.

Hot and cold places

The Earth gets its heat and light from the Sun. The Sun's heat is strongest around the middle of the Earth. At the top and bottom of the Earth, the Sun's rays spread out and it is cold there.

The equator is an imaginary line around the widest part of the Earth. Places near the equator are hot.

Equator

Mount Kilimanjaro in Africa is so high that it always has snow on top – even though it is close to the equator.

Places near the equator that are hot and dry are called deserts. It is hard for trees to grow here.

Hot, wet places near the equator are often covered with forests.

The North and South Poles are icy cold. In some places the ground is covered in snow all year round.

Stormy weather

Storms, floods, long dry spells, or very strong winds can sometimes make the Earth a dangerous place.

A tornado is a tall, thin tube of spinning wind. It stretches from the clouds to the ground. A tornado travels quickly, sucking up almost everything in its path.

Tornadoes sometimes suck up frogs and fish — and drop them in a different place.

Lightning is a bolt of electricity moving from one cloud to another, or from a cloud to the ground. The lightning heats the air around it, making a loud bang. This is called thunder!

Floods happen after heavy rainfall. Streams and rivers burst their banks. Water rushes through towns, over roads and across farmland.

Habitats

The world's plants and animals are well suited to the places in which they live. Their natural homes are called habitats.

Coral reefs are found in tropical seas. The coral animals feed on tiny shellfish. Reefs are also home to brightly coloured fish, jellyfish and starfish.

Penguins live at the cold South Pole. They have a thick layer of fat under their skin to help keep them warm.

The Earth's big region of tropical grassland is called savanna. Grass eaters, such as zebra and antelope, live here.

Many desert animals, such as the meerkat, have long claws for digging. They shelter underground from the hot sun.

The hot, wet rain forests near the equator have a lot of trees and vines. Most rainforest animals live and find food in the trees.

Looking after our world

People everywhere are changing the Earth. Natural habitats are in danger of being lost or ruined forever.

If you destroy an animal's habitat, the animal will die. A lot of plants and animals, such as polar bears, are in danger of dying out forever.

Most of the world's energy comes from fossil fuels, such as coal, oil and natural gas. These fuels can make the air dirty – and supplies are running out.

People are working out ways to get cleaner energy from the wind, the Sun and the waves.

Our waste is buried in huge landfill sites, which can damage the land.

You can reduce waste. Reuse glass bottles and jars, and recycle paper, plastic and metal.

Quiz

Now try this quiz!
All the answers can be found in this book.

What is the Earth surrounded by?

(a) Air
(b) Dust
(c) Sugar

Which is the hottest place inside the Earth?

(a) The mantle
(b) The crust
(c) The core

Magma that has reached the surface of the Earth is called what?

(a) Sand
(b) Lava
(c) Granite

Which are the world's highest mountains?

(a) The Andes
(b) The Rockies
(c) The Himalayas

What is lightning made of?

(a) Electricity
(b) Paper
(c) Metal

Where are coral reefs found?

(a) In rainforests
(b) In tropical seas
(c) In New York

Glossary

Atmosphere   The invisible cloak of air that surrounds the Earth. It is made up of gas, water and dust.

Continent   A large area of land. Continents are often surrounded by seas.

Equator   An imaginary line that runs around the Earth, halfway between the North Pole and the South Pole.

Fossil fuel   A fuel that has been made from the remains of plants or animals. Coal, oil and natural gas are fossil fuels.

Habitat   The natural home of a plant or animal.

Mineral	A chemical substance that can be found in the Earth's crust. Minerals are the building blocks of rocks.
Plates	The huge pieces of rock that make up the Earth's surface.
Planet	A large ball of rock or gas that travels round a star.
Poles	The areas at the very top and bottom of the Earth.

Index

n

natural gas 25
North and South Poles 19, 23
Northern Hemisphere 7

o

oil 25

p

penguins 23
planet Earth 6-7
plates 10, 11, 14
polar bears 24

r

rainforests 23
recycling 25
rivers 15, 21
rocks 6, 8, 12, 15, 16-17

s

savanna 23
seasons 7
silver 17
snow 19
soil 6, 17
Southern Hemisphere 7
spinning 6
storms 20-21

Sun 6, 7, 18

t

thunder 21
tilting 7
tornadoes 20, 21
tropical seas 22

v

valleys 14, 15
volcanoes 12-13, 15

w

waste 25
water 6, 21, 22

z

zebra 23

Acknowledgements

t=top, c=centre, b=bottom, r=right, l=left

Artwork supplied through the Art Agency by artists including
Peter Bull and Myke Taylor

1 Digital Vision, 3 Digital Vision, 4 Oleg Fedorenko/Dreamstime.com,
5tl Michael S. Yamashita/Corbis, 5br, 6 Digital Vision, 7 Doable/
amanaimages/Corbis, 9tr Visuals Unlimited/Corbis, 9lc Millan/
Dreamstme.com 11r Mark Downey / Lucid Images/Corbis, 11l Michael
S. Yamashita/Corbis, 12-13 Jim Sugar/Corbis, 13tl Gary Braasch/
Corbis, 13br Roger Messmeyer/Corbis, 14-15 Galen Rowell/Corbis, 15tr
Rey Rojo/iStockphoto, 15 mr RollingEarth/iStockphoto, 16-17 Herbert
Spichtinger/zefa/Corbis, 16b Joel W. Rogers/Corbis, 17tl Gerald Favre/
Corbis, 17tr Oleg Fedorenko/Dreamstime.com, 17b Ann Johansson/
Corbis, 18b Layne Kennedy/Corbis, 18t Digital Vision, 19tr Digital Vision,
19br Dennis Sabo/Dreamstime, 20-21 Aaron Horowitz/Corbis, 21tr Alle/
Dreamstime, 21mr Reuters/Corbis, 21bl Tacrafts/Dreamstime, 22 Gray
Hardel/Corbis, 23tl Paul Souders/Corbis, 23tr DLILLC/Corbis, 23bl
Nigel J. Dennis; Gallo Images/Corbis, 23br Tom Brakefield/Corbis, 24t
Jan Will/iStockphoto, 24b Wayne Lawler; Ecoscene/Corbis, 25cr (lower)
DLILLC/Corbis, 25br Rtimages/Dreamstime, 29 Digital Vision

Additional images used on sticker sheet: second row, first picture:
David Lloyd/Dreamstime.com